Books have the power to change lives.

SureShot Books Publishing LLC is part of the SureShot 2k family of companies that was founded in 1990 to help inmates & their families by making it possible to improve their lives with the Power of Reading.

Here at SureShot Books, we fervently believe that the fact that you have made a mistake does and should not mean that your life is ruined forever.

We believe that everyone deserves a second chance.

Contact Us with any questions or concerns:
SureShot Books Publishing LLC
P.O. Box 924, Nyack, New York 10960
845.675.7505
Email Us:
info@sureshotbooks.com

INMATE NAME

INMATE NUMBER

CONTACT INFO

NAME:

ADDRESS:

PHONE: NOTE:

EMAIL: WEBSITE:

NAME:

ADDRESS:

PHONE: NOTE:

EMAIL: WEBSITE:

NAME:

ADDRESS:

PHONE: NOTE:

EMAIL: WEBSITE:

NAME:

ADDRESS:

PHONE: NOTE:

EMAIL: WEBSITE:

CONTACT INFO

NAME:

ADDRESS:

PHONE:

NOTE:

EMAIL:

WEBSITE:

NAME:

ADDRESS:

PHONE:

NOTE:

EMAIL:

WEBSITE:

NAME:

ADDRESS:

PHONE:

NOTE:

EMAIL:

WEBSITE:

NAME:

ADDRESS:

PHONE:

NOTE:

EMAIL:

WEBSITE:

CONTACT INFO

NAME:

ADDRESS:

PHONE:

EMAIL:

NOTE:

WEBSITE:

NAME:

ADDRESS:

PHONE:

EMAIL:

NOTE:

WEBSITE:

NAME:

ADDRESS:

PHONE:

EMAIL:

NOTE:

WEBSITE:

NAME:

ADDRESS:

PHONE:

EMAIL:

NOTE:

WEBSITE:

CONTACT INFO

NAME:

ADDRESS:

PHONE: NOTE:

EMAIL: WEBSITE:

NAME:

ADDRESS:

PHONE: NOTE:

EMAIL: WEBSITE:

NAME:

ADDRESS:

PHONE: NOTE:

EMAIL: WEBSITE:

NAME:

ADDRESS:

PHONE: NOTE:

EMAIL: WEBSITE:

INTRODUCTION:

Welcome to the "Islamic Finance Planner: Budgeting for Barakah." In the realm of personal finance, the principles of Islamic finance offer a unique and ethically grounded approach to managing wealth. This planner is designed to be your companion on a journey toward financial success while adhering to the principles of Sharia.

Understanding Islamic Finance:

Islamic finance is rooted in the teachings of Islam, emphasizing ethical practices, fairness, and social responsibility. It goes beyond mere monetary transactions, encouraging a holistic and purposeful approach to wealth management.

The Importance of Aligning with Islamic Principles:

Aligning your financial practices with Islamic principles not only ensures ethical conduct but also invites blessings (barakah) into your financial endeavors. It promotes the responsible use of wealth, encourages charitable giving, and fosters a sense of community well-being.

INTRODUCTION:

Why This Planner Matters:
This planner is not just about numbers; it's about cultivating a mindset of gratitude, responsibility, and abundance. It provides practical tools to help you budget effectively, save with purpose, and navigate the financial landscape in a way that resonates with your Islamic values.

What to Expect:
Inside these pages, you'll find monthly budgeting templates, savings trackers, and valuable tips to guide you on your financial journey. Whether you're new to Islamic finance or seeking to deepen your understanding, this planner is a resource for everyone committed to financial well-being rooted in ethical principles.

As you embark on this path, may your financial pursuits be blessed with abundance, and may this planner be a source of guidance and inspiration in your pursuit of barakah. Welcome to a journey of purposeful and Islamic-centric financial planning!

INTRODUCTION:

The Purpose of the Planner:
The primary purpose of this planner is to empower you in managing your finances in a manner that aligns with Islamic principles. It goes beyond traditional financial planning, emphasizing ethical considerations, responsible wealth management, and the pursuit of blessings (barakah) in your financial journey.

Goals of the Planner:
Alignment with Islamic Principles:
Foster a deep understanding of Islamic finance principles and their application in everyday financial decisions.

Practical Budgeting:
Provide practical tools and templates for effective budgeting that resonate with Islamic values, ensuring responsible spending and saving.

Cultivating Barakah:
Encourage a mindset of gratitude, responsibility, and intentionality in financial matters to attract the blessings of barakah into your life.

INTRODUCTION:

Holistic Financial Well-Being:
Address various aspects of financial well-being, including savings, debt management, and charitable giving, within the framework of Islamic ethics.

Educational Resource:
Serve as an educational resource, guiding both beginners and those well-versed in Islamic finance toward a more purposeful and fulfilling financial life.

Reflective Journey:
Promote self-reflection on financial habits, goals, and the broader significance of wealth in the context of Islamic teachings.

What to Expect:

Monthly Budgeting Templates:
Structured templates to help you plan and monitor your monthly income and expenses.

Savings Trackers:
Tools to set and track savings goals in alignment with your financial objectives.

No amount of materialism, money and power you consume can bring you happiness & contentment, if you have lost touched with the creator.

"You know what the Quran teaches me?
The Quran teaches me that an
incredibly wealthy man can be a failure
(Firaun) and a homeless man can be
successful (Prophet Ibrahim).
It teaches me that success has nothing
to do with wealth and failure has
nothing to do with poverty."

-Ustadh Nouman Ali Khan 

ISLAMIC FINANCE PRINCIPLES:

In the realm of financial management, Islamic finance stands as a distinct and ethically grounded system, guided by principles derived from Islamic law (Sharia). Understanding these principles is pivotal to aligning one's financial practices with ethical considerations and fostering a sense of barakah (blessings). Here, we delve into the key tenets of Islamic finance:

1. Sharia Compliance:

At the core of Islamic finance is adherence to Sharia, the Islamic legal framework. All financial transactions must comply with Sharia principles, which prohibit certain practices such as usury (riba), uncertainty (gharar), and investments in prohibited industries like gambling and alcohol.

2. Ethical Investing:

Islamic finance encourages ethical investments that align with Islamic values. Investments in businesses involved in activities deemed unethical or harmful to society are avoided, promoting social responsibility and sustainability.

3. Risk-Sharing and Profit-and-Loss Sharing:

Islamic finance promotes risk-sharing and profit-and-loss sharing arrangements. In transactions such as Mudarabah (profit-sharing) and Musharakah (partnership), both parties share in the risks and rewards, fostering a fair and just

ISLAMIC FINANCE PRINCIPLES:

financial system.

4. Zakat and Charity:
The payment of Zakat, a mandatory form of almsgiving, is a fundamental principle in Islamic finance. A percentage of one's wealth is given annually to support the less fortunate, ensuring wealth distribution and social welfare.

5. Interest-Free Transactions:
Riba, or usury/interest, is strictly prohibited in Islamic finance. Transactions must be interest-free to ensure fairness and to prevent the exploitation of borrowers.

6. Tangible Asset Backing:
Islamic finance often involves transactions backed by tangible assets. For example, in Islamic mortgages (Murabaha), the property serves as collateral, ensuring a tangible basis for financial transactions.

7. Avoidance of Speculation (Gharar):
Transactions involving excessive uncertainty or speculation (gharar) are discouraged. Islamic finance aims to promote transparency and fairness in all dealings.

8. Debt Management:
While borrowing is allowed in Islam, it should be done

ISLAMIC FINANCE PRINCIPLES:

responsibly. Excessive debt is discouraged, and specific rules govern how debts should be structured and repaid to avoid undue burden on the borrower.

9. Halal Investments:

Investments in businesses that deal with activities such as gambling, alcohol, and pork are prohibited. Islamic finance encourages investments in halal (permissible) sectors, promoting ethical business practices.

10. Transparent and Fair Contracts:

All financial contracts in Islamic finance must be transparent and fair. Parties involved should have a clear understanding of the terms and conditions, promoting honesty and integrity in financial dealings.

إِنَّمَآ أَمْوَٰلُكُمْ وَأَوْلَٰدُكُمْ فِتْنَةٌ

Your wealth and

children are only a test.

(64:15)

SETTING FINANCIAL GOALS:

Establishing clear and achievable financial goals is a crucial step in navigating the path toward financial success and stability. Whether you're starting your financial journey or reassessing your objectives, thoughtful goal-setting is key. Here's guidance to help you set clear and achievable financial goals:

1. Reflect on Your Values:
Begin by reflecting on your values and priorities. What matters most to you? Your financial goals should align with your values, whether they involve family, education, travel, or charitable contributions.

2. Define Short-Term and Long-Term Goals:
Categorize your goals into short-term (within a year), medium-term (1-5 years), and long-term (5+ years). This division helps create a timeline for achieving various objectives.

3. Make Your Goals Specific:
The more specific your goals, the easier it is to work toward them. Instead of a general goal like "save money," specify an amount and a timeframe, such as "save $5,000 for an emergency fund in the next 12 months."

SETTING FINANCIAL GOALS:

4. Prioritize Your Goals:

Prioritization is essential when you have multiple financial goals. Identify the most pressing and impactful goals to focus on first.

5. Set Measurable Targets:

Create measurable targets for each goal. For instance, if your goal is to pay off debt, specify the amount and the timeframe in which you aim to achieve it.

6. Consider SMART Criteria:

Use the SMART criteria for goal-setting: Specific, Measurable, Achievable, Relevant, and Time-bound. This framework ensures that your goals are well-defined and realistic.

7. Account for Life Changes:

Life is dynamic, and circumstances change. Factor in potential life changes like job transitions, family additions, or unexpected expenses when setting your goals.

8. Balance Your Goals:

Strike a balance between short-term gratification and long-term stability. Allocating resources to both immediate needs and future goals creates a well-rounded financial plan.

SETTING FINANCIAL GOALS:

9. Create a Budget:
A budget is a powerful tool for achieving financial goals. It helps you allocate funds toward your priorities and identify areas where adjustments may be needed.

10. Review and Adjust Regularly:
Regularly review your financial goals and assess your progress. Life circumstances, priorities, and financial situations change. Be flexible and adjust your goals accordingly.

11. Celebrate Milestones:
Celebrate your achievements along the way, whether big or small. Acknowledging milestones keeps you motivated and reinforces positive financial habits.

12. Seek Professional Advice:
If needed, consider consulting with a financial advisor. They can provide guidance tailored to your specific situation, helping you refine your goals and create a realistic plan.

Remember that financial goals are personal, and there's no one-size-fits-all approach. Tailor your goals to your unique circumstances, and be patient with the process. By setting clear, achievable goals and staying committed to them, you'll pave the way for a more secure and fulfilling financial future.

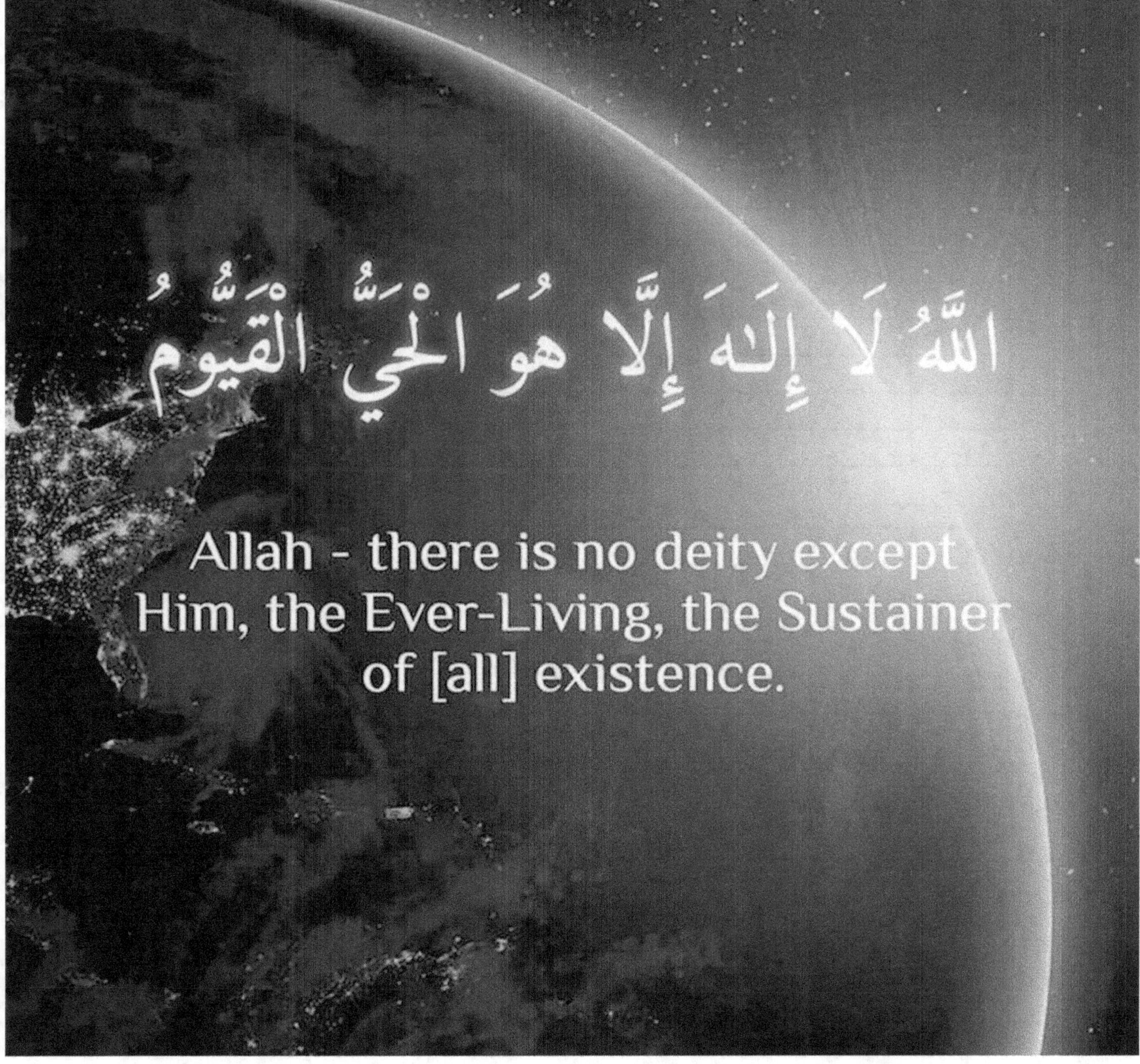

اللَّهُ لَا إِلَهَ إِلَّا هُوَ الْحَيُّ الْقَيُّومُ
Allah - there is no deity except Him, the Ever-Living, the Sustainer of [all] existence.

MONTHLY BUDGET PLANNER

Budget Goal: ________________________   Month: ________________________

Income

Date	Description	Amount
Total		

Fixed Expenses

Date	Description	Amount
Total		

Other Expenses

Date	Description	Amount
Total		

Bills

Date	Description	Amount
Total		

Recap

	Goal	Actual	Difference
Earnt			
Spent			
Debt			
Saved			

notes

MONTHLY BUDGET PLANNER

Budget Goal: _______________________   Month: _______________________

Income

Date	Description	Amount
Total		

Fixed Expenses

Date	Description	Amount
Total		

Other Expenses

Date	Description	Amount
Total		

Bills

Date	Description	Amount
Total		

Recap

	Goal	Actual	Difference
Earnt			
Spent			
Debt			
Saved			

notes

MONTHLY BUDGET PLANNER

Budget Goal: _______________________   Month: _______________________

Income

Date	Description	Amount
Total		

Fixed Expenses

Date	Description	Amount
Total		

Other Expenses

Date	Description	Amount
Total		

Bills

Date	Description	Amount
Total		

Recap

	Goal	Actual	Difference
Earnt			
Spent			
Debt			
Saved			

notes

MONTHLY BUDGET PLANNER

Budget Goal: _________________________   Month: _________________________

Income

Date	Description	Amount
Total		

Fixed Expenses

Date	Description	Amount
Total		

Other Expenses

Date	Description	Amount
Total		

Bills

Date	Description	Amount
Total		

Recap

	Goal	Actual	Difference
Earnt			
Spent			
Debt			
Saved			

notes

MONTHLY BUDGET PLANNER

Budget Goal: _______________________   Month: _______________________

Income

Date	Description	Amount
Total		

Fixed Expenses

Date	Description	Amount
Total		

Other Expenses

Date	Description	Amount
Total		

Bills

Date	Description	Amount
Total		

Recap

	Goal	Actual	Difference
Earnt			
Spent			
Debt			
Saved			

notes

MONTHLY BUDGET PLANNER

Budget Goal: _________________________   Month: _________________________

Income

Date	Description	Amount
Total		

Fixed Expenses

Date	Description	Amount
Total		

Other Expenses

Date	Description	Amount
Total		

Bills

Date	Description	Amount
Total		

Recap

	Goal	Actual	Difference
Earnt			
Spent			
Debt			
Saved			

notes

MONTHLY BUDGET PLANNER

Budget Goal: _________________________   Month: _________________________

Income

Date	Description	Amount
Total		

Fixed Expenses

Date	Description	Amount
Total		

Other Expenses

Date	Description	Amount
Total		

Bills

Date	Description	Amount
Total		

Recap

	Goal	Actual	Difference
Earnt			
Spent			
Debt			
Saved			

notes

MONTHLY BUDGET PLANNER

Budget Goal: _______________________   Month: _______________________

Income

Date	Description	Amount
Total		

Fixed Expenses

Date	Description	Amount
Total		

Other Expenses

Date	Description	Amount
Total		

Bills

Date	Description	Amount
Total		

Recap

	Goal	Actual	Difference
Earnt			
Spent			
Debt			
Saved			

notes

MONTHLY BUDGET PLANNER

Budget Goal: _______________________

Month: _______________________

Income

Date	Description	Amount
Total		

Fixed Expenses

Date	Description	Amount
Total		

Other Expenses

Date	Description	Amount
Total		

Bills

Date	Description	Amount
Total		

Recap

	Goal	Actual	Difference
Earnt			
Spent			
Debt			
Saved			

notes

MONTHLY BUDGET PLANNER

Budget Goal: _______________________   Month: _______________________

Income

Date	Description	Amount
Total		

Fixed Expenses

Date	Description	Amount
Total		

Other Expenses

Date	Description	Amount
Total		

Bills

Date	Description	Amount
Total		

Recap

	Goal	Actual	Difference
Earnt			
Spent			
Debt			
Saved			

notes

MONTHLY BUDGET PLANNER

Budget Goal: ___________________   Month: ___________________

Income

Date	Description	Amount
Total		

Fixed Expenses

Date	Description	Amount
Total		

Other Expenses

Date	Description	Amount
Total		

Bills

Date	Description	Amount
Total		

Recap

	Goal	Actual	Difference
Earnt			
Spent			
Debt			
Saved			

notes

MONTHLY BUDGET PLANNER

Budget Goal: ________________________   **Month:** ________________________

Income

Date	Description	Amount
Total		

Fixed Expenses

Date	Description	Amount
Total		

Other Expenses

Date	Description	Amount
Total		

Bills

Date	Description	Amount
Total		

Recap

	Goal	Actual	Difference
Earnt			
Spent			
Debt			
Saved			

notes

Allahoumabareek 🤍
@dikra_msahal

سَيَجْعَلُ ٱللَّهُ بَعْدَ عُسْرٍ يُسْرًا
Allah will bring about, after hardship, ease.
@TaqvaOfficial
Quran 65:7

SAVING TRACKER

SAVING FOR:

NOTES:

STARTING BALANCE:

SAVINGS GOAL:

DEPOSIT: DATE:

TOTAL =

notes

SAVING TRACKER

SAVING FOR:

NOTES:

STARTING BALANCE:

SAVINGS GOAL:

DEPOSIT: DATE:

TOTAL =

notes

SAVING TRACKER

SAVING FOR:

NOTES:

STARTING BALANCE:

SAVINGS GOAL:

DEPOSIT: DATE:

TOTAL =

notes

SAVING TRACKER

SAVING FOR:

NOTES:

STARTING BALANCE:

SAVINGS GOAL:

DEPOSIT: DATE:

TOTAL =

notes

SAVING TRACKER

SAVING FOR:

NOTES:

STARTING BALANCE:

SAVINGS GOAL:

DEPOSIT: DATE:

TOTAL =

notes

SAVING TRACKER

SAVING FOR:

NOTES:

STARTING BALANCE:

SAVINGS GOAL:

DEPOSIT:

DATE:

TOTAL =

notes

SAVING TRACKER

SAVING FOR:

NOTES:

STARTING BALANCE:

SAVINGS GOAL:

DEPOSIT:

DATE:

TOTAL =

notes

SAVING TRACKER

SAVING FOR:

NOTES:

STARTING BALANCE:

SAVINGS GOAL:

DEPOSIT: DATE:

TOTAL =

notes

SAVING TRACKER

SAVING FOR:

NOTES:

STARTING BALANCE:

SAVINGS GOAL:

DEPOSIT: DATE:

TOTAL =

notes

SAVING TRACKER

SAVING FOR:

NOTES:

STARTING BALANCE:

SAVINGS GOAL:

DEPOSIT: DATE:

TOTAL =

notes

SAVING TRACKER

SAVING FOR:

NOTES:

STARTING BALANCE:

SAVINGS GOAL:

DEPOSIT:

DATE:

TOTAL =

notes

SAVING TRACKER

SAVING FOR:

NOTES:

STARTING BALANCE:

SAVINGS GOAL:

DEPOSIT: DATE:

TOTAL =

notes

DEBT REPAYMENT PLAN:

Managing and repaying debts in a Sharia-compliant manner is an essential aspect of responsible financial management in Islamic finance. Here's a guide to help you navigate the process:

1. Assess Your Debt Situation:
List All Debts:
Make a comprehensive list of all your debts, including the creditor, outstanding balance, interest rates (if any), and repayment terms.

2. Prioritize Your Debts:
Identify High-Priority Debts:
Prioritize debts based on factors such as interest rates, outstanding balances, and the nature of the debt (e.g., essential living expenses).

3. Negotiate Sharia-Compliant Terms:
Engage with Creditors:
If possible, negotiate with creditors for more favorable and Sharia-compliant terms. Discuss options such as reducing interest rates, extending repayment periods, or exploring debt restructuring.

DEBT REPAYMENT PLAN:

4. Develop a Repayment Plan:
Determine Affordable Payments:
Assess your financial situation and determine how much you can realistically afford to allocate toward debt repayment each month.

5. Utilize Islamic Financing Alternatives:
Consider Islamic Finance Products:
Explore Sharia-compliant financing options such as Mudarabah or Murabaha when seeking additional financial support. Ensure that any new financing aligns with Islamic principles.

6. Allocate Extra Funds to High-Priority Debts:
Snowball or Avalanche Method:
Consider popular debt repayment methods like the snowball or avalanche method. Allocate extra funds to either the smallest debt (snowball) or the debt with the highest interest rate (avalanche) while making minimum payments on other debts.

7. Monitor Progress:
Regularly Review and Adjust:
Monitor your progress regularly and adjust your repayment plan as needed. Celebrate milestones, and stay motivated by witnessing the reduction of debt over time.

DEBT REPAYMENT PLAN:

8. Seek Financial Counseling:
Consult with Islamic Financial Advisors:
If needed, seek guidance from Islamic financial advisors. They can provide insights tailored to your situation and offer advice on managing debts while adhering to Sharia principles.

9. Avoid New Interest-Bearing Debts:
Commit to Sharia Principles:
Refrain from taking on new debts that involve interest. Stick to financial practices that align with Islamic principles to prevent further financial burdens.

10. Involve Charity in Your Plan:
Zakat Allocation:
Consider allocating a portion of your income designated for Zakat to help those in need. This practice aligns with Islamic teachings and contributes to a more holistic financial plan.

11. Seek Forgiveness:
Seek Allah's Forgiveness:
While working diligently to repay debts, seek forgiveness from Allah. Sincerely repent for any financial mistakes and commit to ethical financial practices moving forward.

What kind of wealth should we acquire?

He replied: Let one of you acquire: A thankful heart, a tongue that remembers Allah, and a believing wife who will aid him with regard to the Hereafter.

Debt Payoff Tracker

Debt:

Month:

	Beg Balance				
	Payment				
	Balance				
	Payment				
	Balance				
	Payment				
	Balance				
	Payment				
	Balance				
	Payment				
	Balance				
	Payment				
	Balance				
	Payment				
	Balance				
	Payment				
	Balance				
	Payment				
	Balance				
	Payment				
	Balance				
	Payment				
	Balance				
	Payment				
	End Balance				

Debt Payoff Tracker

Month:

Debt:

	Beg Balance				
	Payment				
	Balance				
	Payment				
	Balance				
	Payment				
	Balance				
	Payment				
	Balance				
	Payment				
	Balance				
	Payment				
	Balance				
	Payment				
	Balance				
	Payment				
	Balance				
	Payment				
	Balance				
	Payment				
	Balance				
	Payment				
	Balance				
	Payment				
	End Balance				

Debt Payoff Tracker

Debt:

Month:

	Beg Balance				
	Payment				
	Balance				
	Payment				
	Balance				
	Payment				
	Balance				
	Payment				
	Balance				
	Payment				
	Balance				
	Payment				
	Balance				
	Payment				
	Balance				
	Payment				
	Balance				
	Payment				
	Balance				
	Payment				
	Balance				
	Payment				
	Balance				
	Payment				
	End Balance				

Debt *Payoff* Tracker

Debt:

Month:

	Beg Balance				
	Payment				
	Balance				
	Payment				
	Balance				
	Payment				
	Balance				
	Payment				
	Balance				
	Payment				
	Balance				
	Payment				
	Balance				
	Payment				
	Balance				
	Payment				
	Balance				
	Payment				
	Balance				
	Payment				
	Balance				
	Payment				
	Balance				
	Payment				
	End Balance				

Debt Payoff Tracker

Month:

Debt:

	Beg Balance				
	Payment				
	Balance				
	Payment				
	Balance				
	Payment				
	Balance				
	Payment				
	Balance				
	Payment				
	Balance				
	Payment				
	Balance				
	Payment				
	Balance				
	Payment				
	Balance				
	Payment				
	Balance				
	Payment				
	Balance				
	Payment				
	Balance				
	Payment				
	End Balance				

Debt Payoff Tracker

Debt:

Month:

	Beg Balance				
	Payment				
	Balance				
	Payment				
	Balance				
	Payment				
	Balance				
	Payment				
	Balance				
	Payment				
	Balance				
	Payment				
	Balance				
	Payment				
	Balance				
	Payment				
	Balance				
	Payment				
	Balance				
	Payment				
	Balance				
	Payment				
	Balance				
	Payment				
	End Balance				

Debt Payoff Tracker

Debt:

Month:

	Beg Balance				
	Payment				
	Balance				
	Payment				
	Balance				
	Payment				
	Balance				
	Payment				
	Balance				
	Payment				
	Balance				
	Payment				
	Balance				
	Payment				
	Balance				
	Payment				
	Balance				
	Payment				
	Balance				
	Payment				
	Balance				
	Payment				
	Balance				
	Payment				
	End Balance				

Debt Payoff Tracker

Month:

Debt:

	Beg Balance				
	Payment				
	Balance				
	Payment				
	Balance				
	Payment				
	Balance				
	Payment				
	Balance				
	Payment				
	Balance				
	Payment				
	Balance				
	Payment				
	Balance				
	Payment				
	Balance				
	Payment				
	Balance				
	Payment				
	Balance				
	Payment				
	Balance				
	Payment				
	End Balance				

Debt Payoff Tracker

Debt:

Month:

	Beg Balance				
	Payment				
	Balance				
	Payment				
	Balance				
	Payment				
	Balance				
	Payment				
	Balance				
	Payment				
	Balance				
	Payment				
	Balance				
	Payment				
	Balance				
	Payment				
	Balance				
	Payment				
	Balance				
	Payment				
	Balance				
	Payment				
	Balance				
	Payment				
	End Balance				

Debt Payoff Tracker

Debt:

Month:

	Beg Balance				
	Payment				
	Balance				
	Payment				
	Balance				
	Payment				
	Balance				
	Payment				
	Balance				
	Payment				
	Balance				
	Payment				
	Balance				
	Payment				
	Balance				
	Payment				
	Balance				
	Payment				
	Balance				
	Payment				
	Balance				
	Payment				
	Balance				
	Payment				
	End Balance				

Debt Payoff Tracker

Month:

Debt: ⬚ ⬚ ⬚ ⬚

	Beg Balance				
	Payment				
	Balance				
	Payment				
	Balance				
	Payment				
	Balance				
	Payment				
	Balance				
	Payment				
	Balance				
	Payment				
	Balance				
	Payment				
	Balance				
	Payment				
	Balance				
	Payment				
	Balance				
	Payment				
	Balance				
	Payment				
	Balance				
	Payment				
	End Balance				

Debt Payoff Tracker

Debt:

Month:

	Beg Balance				
	Payment				
	Balance				
	Payment				
	Balance				
	Payment				
	Balance				
	Payment				
	Balance				
	Payment				
	Balance				
	Payment				
	Balance				
	Payment				
	Balance				
	Payment				
	Balance				
	Payment				
	Balance				
	Payment				
	Balance				
	Payment				
	Balance				
	Payment				
	End Balance				

TIPS FOR FINANCIAL SUCCESS:

Achieving financial success involves a combination of strategic planning, disciplined saving, and halal financial choices. Here are practical tips to guide you on your journey to financial well-being:

1. Set Clear Financial Goals:
Define short-term and long-term financial goals. Having clear objectives helps you stay focused and motivated.

2. Create and Stick to a Budget:
Develop a budget that aligns with your goals. Track your income, expenses, and allocate funds wisely to avoid unnecessary debt.

3. Save Regularly:
Cultivate a habit of saving. Set aside a portion of your income each month for emergencies, future goals, and unexpected expenses.

4. Embrace Halal Investments:
Explore halal investment options such as Islamic mutual funds, real estate, or ethical businesses. Ensure your investments align with Islamic principles.

5. Educate Yourself:
Stay informed about financial matters. Continuous learning

TIPS FOR FINANCIAL SUCCESS:

empowers you to make informed and wise financial decisions.

6. Avoid Riba (Interest):

Refrain from engaging in transactions that involve interest (riba). Seek halal financing alternatives and uphold ethical financial practices.

7. Be Mindful of Spending:

Practice mindful spending. Differentiate between needs and wants, and prioritize essential expenses over non-essential ones.

8. Diversify Your Income Streams:

Explore multiple sources of income to enhance financial stability. Diversification minimizes risks and opens up new opportunities.

9. Clear Debts Strategically:

Prioritize and systematically pay off debts. Adopt a strategic approach, focusing on high-interest debts first.

10. Practice Gratitude:

Cultivate gratitude for what you have. A positive mindset enhances your financial well-being and reduces the desire for unnecessary expenditures.

TIPS FOR FINANCIAL SUCCESS:

11. Plan for Retirement:
Start planning for retirement early. Consider halal retirement savings options to secure your financial future.

12. Give to Charity:
Contribute to charitable causes regularly. Zakat and sadaqah not only fulfill a religious obligation but also purify your wealth.

13. Live Below Your Means:
Avoid excessive spending and live below your means. This practice allows for greater financial flexibility and savings.

14. Review and Adjust:
Regularly review your financial plan and adjust it as needed. Life circumstances change, and your financial strategy should adapt accordingly.

15. Seek Professional Advice:
Consult with Islamic financial advisors if needed. They can provide tailored guidance and help you make decisions aligned with Sharia principles.

وَاصْبِرْ عَلَىٰ مَا أَصَابَكَ ۜ

Endure with patience whatever misfortune strikes you.

Surah Luqman | v. 17

Those who spend on charity
will be richly rewarded.

[Surah Al Hadid: 10]

notes

The Prophet (ﷺ) said,

"Charity does not decrease wealth."

(Muslim)

notes

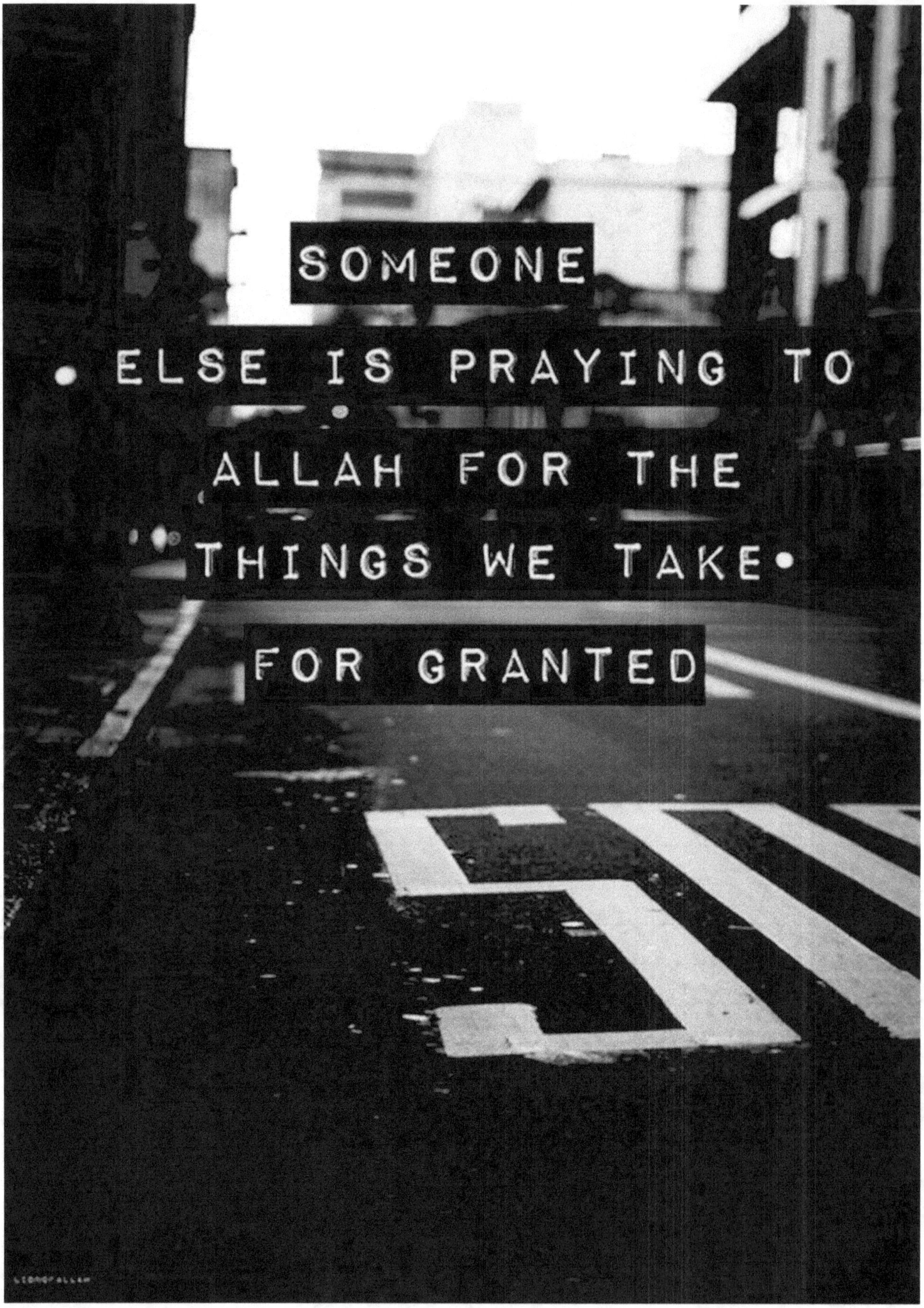

SOMEONE
ELSE IS PRAYING TO
ALLAH FOR THE
THINGS WE TAKE
FOR GRANTED

notes

وَاللَّهُ يُضَاعِفُ لِمَن يَشَاءُ

And Allah multiplies [His reward]
for whom He wills

[2:261] @HopefulRepenter

notes

وَٱصْبِرْ عَلَىٰ مَا يَقُولُونَ
وَٱهْجُرْهُمْ هَجْرًا جَمِيلًا

And be patient over what they say
and avoid them with gracious avoidance.
[73:10]

notes

اَللّٰهُمَّ اكْفِنِىْ بِحَلَالِكَ عَنْ حَرَامِكَ

وَاَغْنِنِىْ بِفَضْلِكَ عَمَّنْ سِوَاكَ

O Allah! Suffice me with Your
halal (lawful) and (save me)
from Your haram (unlawful),
and enrich me with Your favours
so that I am not dependent
upon anyone except You.

Tirmidhi

notes

Harsh Truth

HARAM is HARAM
Even if it's "Culture"

HALAL is HALAL
Even if it's "Mocked"

FARD is FARD
Even if it doesn't fit your "Schedule"

SHIRK is SHIRK
Even if it's "Out of respect"

Wrong is wrong even if everyone is doing it,
Right is right even if no one is doing it.

@theartofelegance

notes

The pure hearts of the servants
are places that Allah, the Glorified, looks upon;
so whoever purifies his heart, He will look upon it.
-Imam Ali (as)
Ghorar al-Hikam

notes

The Prophet ﷺ said,

"Wealth is not in having many possessions, but rather (true) wealth is feeling sufficiency in the soul."

- Sahih al Bukhari 6446

notes

وَقَالَ رَبُّكُمُ ادْعُونِي أَسْتَجِبْ لَكُمْ

And your Lord says,
"Call upon Me; I will respond to you."

Quran 40:60

notes

Dua for Wealth, Money and Good House

اللَّهُمَّ اغْفِرْ لِي ذَنْبِي وَوَسِّعْ لِي فِي دَارِى وَبَارِكْ لِي فِي رِزْقِ *

ALLAHUMMAGHFIRLI DHANBI,
WA WASSI LI FI DARI, WA BARIK
LI FI RIZQI

"O ALLAH, FORGIVE MY SINS, EXPAND MY
ABODE, AND BLESS ME IN MY
PROVISION."

AL-SUNAN AL-KUBRA LIL-NASĀ'Ī 9514
GRADE: SAHIH

notes

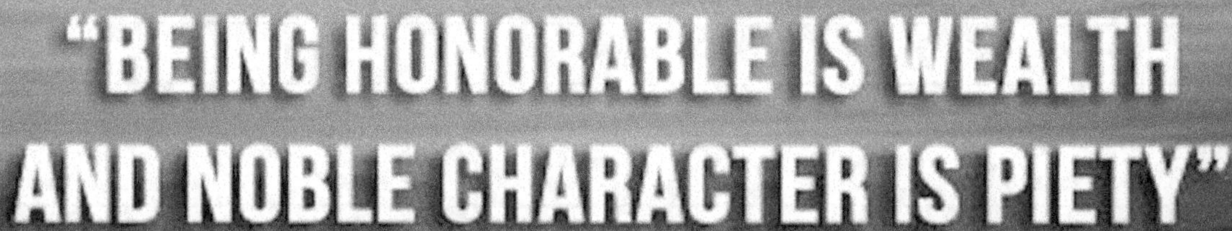

"BEING HONORABLE IS WEALTH
AND NOBLE CHARACTER IS PIETY"
Sunan Ibn Majah (hasan)
teachermuhammad.tumblr.com

notes

Ya Allah
Don't let me be away from You even for a
blink of an eye.
Unfolded Guidance

notes

Open your own convenient and private SureShot Books Publishing Book Account

Convenient for you:

Because we understand the process it takes to forward funds from your inmate account and then have a check mailed to us. You send in a payment which will be added to your account which will be tracked by your Inmate I.D. Number.

So, when we showcase our NEW HOTTEST products you will have funds available for an immediate purchase.

Easier for your family and private for you:

Your family & friends load funds on your inmate account online at **www.sureshotbooks.com**

You order the exact books and magazines you want and your selection is private. You can place orders via email or by using our mail-in order forms.

Email us (or have your loved ones email us) to open your account today!

info@sureshotbooks.com

SureShot Books is on:
SmartJailMail / JPay EMessaging / Corrlinks / Getting out / ConnectNetwork.com Access Corrections / Securus